Alice Korach

Alice Korach is the founding editor of Bead&Button Magazine. Her idea in starting the magazine was that there were many people like her who wanted to know how beautiful beadwork was created, and she was right!

From childhood on, Alice practiced almost all forms of needle art, taking up beading when she was eight and knitting at eleven. She always loved teaching and sharing her skills and knowledge with others. In her first career, Alice earned a Ph.D. in English literature and became a college professor. The biggest problem with academia for her was that one was required to write uninteresting articles for a limited audience of hostile specialists.

So Alice moved on to Threads Magazine where she was an editor in all areas of fiber arts, particularly knitting, and contributed numerous articles of her own work, most notably, the first article explaining bead knitting since the early years of the 20th century.

Alice always knew that she was a good technician and a skilled designer, but she only gradually learned that she was also an artist when she had the privilege of learning pâte de verre from Donna Milliron. Alice went on to create dozens of unique three-dimensional glass sculptures including figurative, abstract, and floral works. Practicing art in glass freed something within her that has led to an artistic flowering in other forms of bead art as well.

Alice teaches at national conventions and shops, particularly at the 'Bead Needs' shop in Hales Corners, Wisconsin.

www.LostWaxGlass.com
LMK467@earthlink.net   262-650-0574
Alice Korach, 518 McCall St., Waukesha, WI 53186

Diamonds on the Square
Bracelets
pages 6 - 9

Octagon Weave
Bracelet
pages 10 - 13

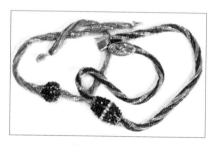

Python Necklace
pages 16 - 19

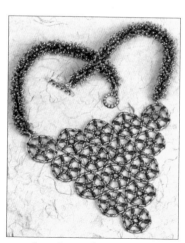

Wheels within Wheels
Necklace
pages 26 - 29

Spiky Spiral Rope
Earrings
pages 14 - 15

Parquet Necklace
pages 20 - 25

Saturn Bracelet
pages 30 - 35

Bead Shapes and Sizes

Unusual beads are great to work with. In this book, I specialized in special shaped beads. They are a lot of fun to work with and give an unusual look to finished jewelry.

Cube Beads: Left, 4mm "oil slick" luster and raku finish matte metallic; center, 3mm silver-lined and matte opaque; right, 2mm raku finish (2 beads); far right, 15/0 round seed beads for comparison.

Cube Beads

Cube beads from Toho are available in four sizes: 1.5mm, 2mm, 3mm, and 4mm. Most Toho cubes have a large slightly diamond-shaped hole; while Miyuki cubes have a large round hole. Finishes range from matte to shiny, opaque, transparent, silver-lined, metallic and luster or aurora borealis (AB).

The 4mm cubes are the easiest size to find. They work well for most projects, but may be a bit too big for a bracelet or a small piece with design details. I really like using the 3mm size because they're small enough to allow room for a bit of embellishment or other design detailing, but they're large enough to present a strong cube shape.

The smallest cubes are about 1.5mm on a side, or about the size of a 15/0 round seed bead. At this size, the cubic form isn't as clear, but if you can find a wide enough range of colors, you can create detailed charted patterns that fit together like a precisely constructed brick road or a micro mosaic.

Triangle Beads: Top left, size 14/0 purple/bronze metallic; center and bottom left, size 11/0 color-lined crystal and "oil slick" luster metallic; top and center right, size 8/0 matte metallic AB and metallic bronze iris; bottom right, size 5/0 color-lined crystal.

Triangle Beads

Triangle beads from Toho are known for their sharp corners; while Miyuki triangles have rounded corners. Toho triangles come in sizes 14/0, 11/0, 8/0, and 5/0. These sizes correspond to round seed beads in terms of the width of the bead across the hole, but they are significantly longer than their round counterparts. You'll find the widest color and finish range in 11/0 triangles, which have been made the longest. But 8/0 triangles are coming along fast, and many come in the same or coordinating colors as 11/0s, which creates a lot of design options.

You'll also find a fair amount of irregularity in a package of triangle beads of any size. In some of the designs in this book, I'll suggest that you carefully sort through your triangle beads for uniform beads, but the "Saturn Bracelet" works best if you take advantage of size variation to pick beads that fill enlarging or shrinking spaces, depending on where you are in the pattern.

Strangely, some colors of triangles have smooth, fire-polished edges, while others seem to be cut like bugles and often present sharp or irregular edges. These are a bit riskier to use, but the colors are irresistible, so cull out those with the roughest edges and reserve them for stringing or fringe.

Threads

You should, of course, use your favorite needles and threads.

Many beaders swear by the strength of Fireline, but I haven't used it since a piece I'd woven on Fireline came apart in a million pieces. I was a Nymo beader until very recently when Toho and Kobayashi both introduced the same new nylon filament thread in slightly different palettes. Toho's thread is called One-G and Kobayashi's is K-O.

The weight is similar to Nymo B, but the thread has a slick coating that causes it to resist fraying without needing any type of thread conditioner (beeswax or Thread Heaven). It also seems to be comparable in strength to Nymo D.

One-G and K-O need to be prestretched before you begin to weave. This thread is very stretchy, so prestretching will prevent your beadwork from becoming loose over time. It also uncoils the thread, which helps minimize tangling.

As with any thread, you should thread the needle with the end that comes off the spool first so you are sewing with the thread's grain to minimize fraying. I am a lazy beader and tend to use excessively long threads. This is a false economy of time because a thread longer than 2 yd. (1.8m) is much more likely to tangle.

If you are using beads with sharp edges, such as crystals or some 11/0 triangles, you may prefer to use Fireline or Power Pro (BeadCats sells a generic version of the latter at a much reduced price). I used One-G for all the projects in this book.

Needles

Since cubes and triangles have large holes, most of the projects in this book can be worked with size 10 English beading needles.

You will need to use a size 12 needle for projects that involve extra thread passes, such as the necklace, embellishment on the "Diamonds in the Square" bracelet, and the "Wheels within Wheels" necklace. "Spiky Spiral Rope" requires a size 13 needle and sometimes the aid of pliers.

Scissors and Glue

My favorite beading scissors are high-quality, Solingen steel manicure scissors. They're very sharp, sturdy, and come to a tiny point. "Stork" embroidery scissors also work well. When cutting off thread tails, use a trick Virginia Blakelock teaches and pull on the thread as you cut it. This stretches it slightly so the end hides inside the last bead. Never cut a thread right after a knot. Pass it through a few beads first.

If you use clear nail polish as glue for your knots, apply a drop from the tip of your beading needle directly on the knot (another Virginia Blakelock trick). Never use the nail polish brush; the solvent could damage bead color or finish.

In the "Saturn Bracelet," I recommend Barge Cement for making the stiff lining rather than E6000. Barge cement is usually available where leather is sold if your bead store doesn't carry it. It doesn't smell as horrible as E6000 and the smell eventually goes away, but the best reason for beaders to use Barge Cement is that it's more flexible and can be sewn through it in a pinch, unlike E6000.

Basic Knots

I've used only two knots in these projects: a surgeon's knot and pairs of half hitches. I tie the surgeon's knot in the reverse order from the method shown in recent books.

My method was taught me by my mother, who learned it from her brother when he was in medical school. It seems logical to me that the longer part of the knot will hold better if it curls around the shorter part. I learned the trick of tying two half hitches in the same place from Dori Jamieson. It's easier and safer than tying a double half hitch, which often tightens too soon. If I want really good hold from half hitches, I'll tie a pair of crossed half hitches.

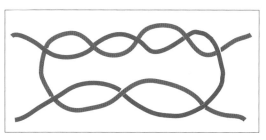

Surgeon's Knot

The surgeon's knot starts like a square knot.

1. Cross the left-hand end on top of the right-hand end, wrap it behind the right-hand cord, and bring it back to the front (lower green line). The right-hand tail (purple) now points left and the left-hand tail points right.

2. Bend the right-hand tail back toward the right and the left-hand tail back toward the left (middle of knot).

3. Cross the tail that's currently on the right (green), over the tail coming from the left (purple).

4. Wrap it behind that tail and pull it through the opening between the step 1 cross and the step 3 cross (this is a square knot).

5. To turn it into a surgeon's knot wrap behind, under, and through to the front again. The result is that the top of the knot curves partway down the sides of the first cross. This makes it more stable and less likely to twist out of the square when you tighten it.

6. Pull the tails in the directions they are pointing to tighten the knot.

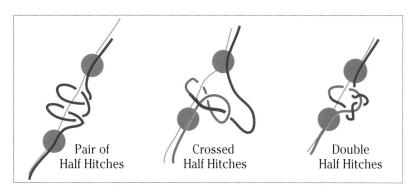

Pair of Half Hitches   Crossed Half Hitches   Double Half Hitches

Half-Hitch Knot

1. For a plain half hitch, bring the needle through a bead. Then sew under the thread between this bead and the next bead. Tighten until a small loop remains.

2. Pass the needle through the loop, going over the thread that you previously sewed under (lower loop in pair of half hitches).

3. Repeat the process for a paired half hitch, at left, that's much more secure than a single half hitch.

4. For a crossed half hitch, repeat step 1 of the plain half hitch. Give the loop on the right a half twist so its sides cross, then sew through it. Tighten carefully so it doesn't lock too soon.

5. Start a double half hitch, right, like a plain half hitch, but sew through the loop twice.

Diamonds on the Square

Make a reversible square-stitch bracelet and appliqué both sides

In August 2002, Anne Nikolai Kloss showed Bead&Button readers how to make reversible triangle-bead bracelets using square stitch. The principle is to use two colors on alternate rows. On one side of the bracelet the wide sides of the odd-numbered row color will face out with just the narrow angle of the even-row color showing between rows. On the other side, the wide sides of the even-numbered row color will be prominent. It's a great effect. So I borrowed Anne's technique for the base bracelet in this project then decided to add my own touch by appliquéing a diamond pattern of the prominent color on each side. The patterns on the two sides are not identical because the number of rows that can be surface embellished decreases by one on each end on the even-numbered side.

When people handle the bracelet, they comment on its scratchy feel since the raised beads have corners. Their first question is why I embellished both sides. What they don't realize until they put on the bracelet is that, when worn, the surface beads lie smoothly against your skin so the bracelet doesn't feel scratchy. Since the benefit of Anne's technique is that you get two bracelets in one, I decided I wanted two embellished bracelets in one as well.

I've used two strongly contrasting colors and finishes for my red and lime green bracelet, but the embellishment is subtle because I've used the same color as the flat triangles on the side. If you'd prefer a more toned-down effect, consider using shades of similar color like my slate and blue-gray bracelet. I made the embellishment more prominent by using shiny metallic luster triangles to embellish the matte gray side and matte metallic luster triangles on the shiny blue side.

Another stunning option would be to use two metallic colors such as golden bronze and silver for a luxurious look of precious metal and to embellish each side with the opposite metal color. A more subtle but equally handsome effect could be produced by using the same color in both matte and shiny finishes.

You might also decide that you only want to embellish one side, leaving the other simple and unadorned. In that case, I recommend that you embellish the odd-numbered row side.

SUPPLIES

20-25g Triangle beads, size 11/0, color A (11T222, metallic bronze-copper or 11T612 matte slate blue)

20-25g Triangle beads, size 11/0, color B (11T24, silver-lined lime or 11T288 color-lined blue-gray/crystal)

8-10g Each of 2 embellishment colors for blue bracelet (11T86 black with rainbow luster and 11T82F matte metallic blue iris)

Beading thread, One-G, burgundy and green; light blue

Beading needles, size 10 and 12 or 13

Magnetic clasp

2 Split rings in matching metal color, 4mm

Split ring pliers optional

HOW-TO

My 99-row bracelet measures 6½" (16.5cm), but I've also included pattern instructions for a 7" (17.8cm) 107-row bracelet and a 7½"(19cm) 115-row version. Every 8 rows, 4 per end, changes the length by ½" (1.3cm).

I recommend that you weave the band in reinforced square stitch, taught to me by Sue Jackson and Wendy Hubick of Hummingbeads, for two reasons. First, reinforced square stitch is so sturdy that you can cut it without losing beads; but more importantly, if you work a long strip of plain square stitch, it will tend to develop a bias. Reinforcing the stitch as you go keeps your strip straight and even.

The bracelet band needs to be slightly longer than you want the finished bracelet because embellishment on both sides decreases its inside diameter.

Reinforced Square-Stitch

Use a size 10 needle to weave the band.

1. Sew a stop bead 8" (20cm) from the end of a 2-yd. (1.8m) length of beading thread (used single).

2. String 7A triangles and pick up 1B (figure 1, coral row and dark blue line at bottom).

3. Sew through the last A in the original direction, that is, toward the B and continue through the B. Tighten the thread to stack the B against the last A (figure 1, blue to purple line, bottom center).

4. Pick up a B and sew through the sixth A toward the seventh. Then sew through the new B away from the previous B.

5. Repeat step 4 to sew a B on top of all the As on row 1. End with your needle exiting the last B and pointing away from the other Bs (figure 1, purple lines).

6. To reinforce the first row, sew through the previous row in the original direction, here top to bottom left (figure 1, yellow line). Then sew through all the beads of the new row, first bead to last bead (figure 1, orange line, bottom to top).

7. With your needle exiting the last new B again, pick up an A for row 3. Sew through the end B in the original stitching direction, here bottom to top, and the new A in its original direction, top to bottom.

8. Pick up another A (figure 1, orange to blue lines at right) and sew through the next B as in step 7, then come back through the A.

9. Repeat down the row until you've sewn an A over the last B (figure 1, blue line at bottom).

10. Reinforce the previous row by sewing through it in the original direction that you added its beads (bottom to top). Sew through all the beads of the last row in the same direction that you added those beads (figure 1, right-hand orange and yellow lines).

11. With your needle exiting the last new bead, pick up the first bead for row 4. Sew 7 Bs to the 7 As the same way you added the row 2 beads.

Then reinforce as in step 6.

12. Add As for every odd-numbered row and Bs for every even-numbered row, reinforcing after completing each row.

Notice that, except for the first and last rows and places where you've added or ended thread, you sew through each bead five times, always going through a bead in the original sewing direction.

13. You will have to add thread. Sew it through 2-4 beads in the next-to-last completed row, going in the same direction as you added beads on that row. Step up to the bead above the one you exited and sew back through 3-4 beads. Step up into the unfinished row and sew through several beads to exit the same one that the old thread is exiting in the same direction. Resume beading with the new thread. After working 4-5 rows, end the old thread by sewing back and forth the same way through a few beads on the first 3 new rows (figure 2). Because this is reinforced square stitch, knots are unnecessary. They could also create problems during embellishing.

14. Work an odd number of rows, preferably 99, 107, or 115, for which I've indicated the place to start embellishment. The clasp will add slightly more than ½" (1.3cm) to the total length of the bracelet.

Figure 1

stop bead

row 1

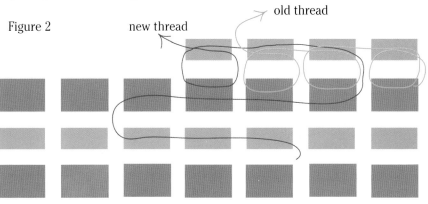

Figure 2

new thread

old thread

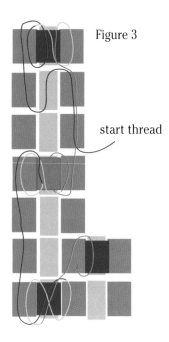

Figure 3

start thread

Embellishment

Embellish the odd-numbered rows side first (the red pattern chart, figure 7, p. 9). For the row counts shown, the pattern will end symmetrically. Use a size 12 or 13 needle for embellishing. Numbers in the directions that follow refer to the 99-row bracelet. Begin the 107- or 115-row bracelets exiting the third or fifth bead on row 1, as indicated on the chart.

Figure 4

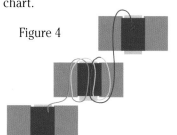

Odd-Numbered Row Side

1. Thread a needle with about 2½ yd. (2.3m) of thread in the embellishment bead color, or use the remaining long thread.

2. To weave a new thread into the beadwork, sew up the third and second beads of row 3, down the second bead of row 2, and up the second and first beads of row 1 (figure 3, dark blue line at top).

3. Pick up a red bead and sew up the first bead of row 1 again. Sew through the embellishment bead again in the original direction. Then sew up the first bead of row 3 (figure 3, yellow line at top).

4. To work the first vertical embellishment row, sew down the first embellishment bead again. Then continue down beads 2, 3, and 4 of row 3 (yellow to light blue line).

5. Pick up a green embellishment bead and sew down bead #4 of row 3 again (figure 3, light blue line).

6. Sew through the embellishment bead again in the original direction. Then sew down bead #4 of row 1 (figure 3, yellow line at center).

7. Sew back up the embellishment bead again then down beads #4-7 of row 1. Pick up the last embellishment bead of the row (figure 3, dark blue line, center to bottom).

8. Sew down bead #7 of row 3 and go through the embellishment bead again in the original direction. Sew down bead #7 of row 1 (figure 3, yellow line at bottom).

9. Sew up the embellishment bead again and continue up bead #6 of row 3 to reach the beginning of the next embellishment. Pick up a new embellishment bead and sew back up bead #6 of row 3 (figure 3, light blue line to arrow).

10. I've found it's easier to embellish along the same diagonal line as it moves up and down across the bracelet. Figure 4 shows this process, beginning with the light blue line as it leaves the bottom of the first vertical row. Work the light blue, yellow, then dark blue lines.

Figure 5

Figure 6

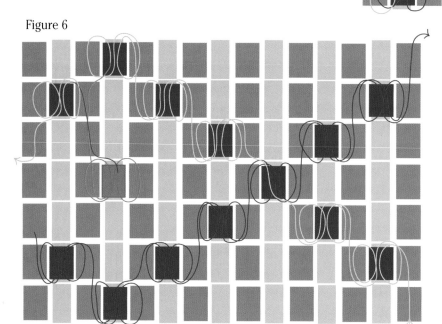

11. When you have added the top or bottom embellishment bead at the other end of the band, go through beads to add the middle green bead, then the other end red bead. Follow that diagonal line back to the start, but detour to add the green center beads when you get to them. Figure 5 shows the most economic pathway for crossing the first diagonal (light blue line), and figure 6 shows how to detour to add the center bead (light blue and blue-green lines).

12. If enough thread remains when you're back at row 1, use it to attach the clasp (see "The clasp" at right.

Even Numbered Row Side

The embellishment beads are sewn between beads on even numbered rows (green chart at right); thus embellishment starts on the second row of the strip. The start row for each size is marked on both charts.

1. Turn the bracelet so the other side is up and the end without a clasp part is row 1. Begin a 2½ yd. thread by sewing up beads in row 4, down row 3, and up row 2 to exit bead #3 and add the first green embellishment bead as you did on the first side in figure 3.

2. Add the other embellishment bead(s) on the first vertical row (between rows 2 and 4 of the band).

3. Then follow a diagonal line to the other end of the band as you did for the red side. Notice that there are 2 horizontal embellishment beads at the wide points of the diamonds and in the centers.

4. Add the embellishment beads on the last row and follow the other vertical line to the start. As before, detour to add the red beads in the centers of the diamonds. I find that it's easiest to add both center beads after adding the first edge bead. Then return to the edge, add the second bead and continue to work on the diagonal. Cross the first diagonal as shown in figure 5.

5. When you get back to the start row, jog over to the end row and attach the other clasp part to the middle bead as described below.

start pattern 99 rows start pattern 115 rows start pattern 107 rows

Figure 7

odd-numbered rows side

even-numbered rows side

start pattern 99 rows start pattern 115 rows start pattern 107 rows

The Clasp

1. Attach a split ring to each of the clasp parts.

2. Exit the middle bead on the first or last row when you have completed the embellishment of a side.

3. Sew through the split ring, then back through the same bead to its other side.

4. Sew through the split ring on the second side of the bead and go back through the bead.

5. Repeat steps 3 and 4 as many times as possible then end the thread in the edge row with 2 pairs of half hitches between beads. Go through the last bead and trim off the excess thread.

Octagon Weave Bracelet

One of the biggest problems with weaving cube beads is those gigantic holes.

Right-angle weave, an enjoyable stitch with a lovely feel and drape, looks especially bad in cubes because all of the cube holes show, not just those on the edge. But I love right-angle weave, so I developed a variation on it that successfully conceals all the cube holes and adds an additional sparkling design element.

I call this stitch "octagon weave" because instead of four beads to a stitch, there are eight, and you work through the piece a second time to pull together all the 4-bead sets made with small beads.

The clasp I used for my bracelet is a cube bead button with a bead loop. If you prefer to use a commercial clasp, by all means, do so.

SUPPLIES

20-30g Cube beads, 3mm (3C43DF matte soft denim)
15g Seed beads, size 11/0 (11R782 luster dark blue)
Beading thread, One-G, dark blue
Beading needles, size 12

HOW-TO

This bracelet is three stitches wide. Work back and forth across the width until the band is the length you want. I've placed the button far enough in from the edge so that the edges meet when the bracelet is fastened.

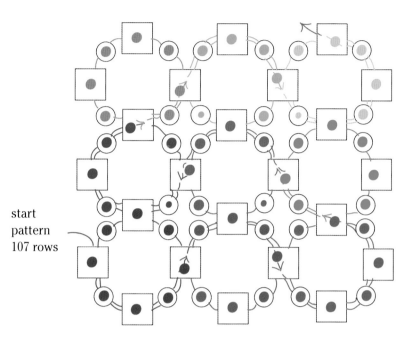

start
pattern
107 rows

Figure 1

Base Layer

You work this layer like David Chatt's single-needle right-angle weave, connecting rows and stitches only through cube beads.

1. Pick up 8 beads, starting with a cube and alternating cube and 11/0. Leave a 15-20" (38-51cm) tail for attaching the button.

2. Tie the 8 beads into a firm ring using 1-2 surgeon's knots. Then sew through the first 5 beads again, exiting the cube opposite the starting cube (figure 1, burgundy beads and line). Notice that you're sewing around these beads in a counter-clockwise direction.

3. Pick up 7 beads, starting with an 11/0 and alternating cubes and 11/0s. After picking up the fourth 11/0, sew through the cube you exited on the previous stitch toward the first bead of the new stitch. Continue through the first 4 beads of the new stitch to exit the middle cube (figure 1, medium red beads and line). Notice that this time you sewed in a clockwise direction; you alternate direction with each stitch.

4. For the third stitch of the first row, again pick up 7 alternating beads, starting with an 11/0, and sew back through the bead you exited on stitch 2 toward the first new bead.

5. To position yourself to begin the next row, sew through 6 of the new beads, exiting the last new cube (figure 1, light red beads and line).

6. For the first stitch of row 2, pick up 7 alternating beads, starting with an 11/0. At the end of the row, continue through the cube you exited on row 1, heading toward the first new bead. Continue through the first 2 new beads, exiting the first cube (figure 1, light blue beads and line).

7. The second stitch is a little tricky. Pick up 5 alternating beads, starting with an 11/0. Then go through the top cube on the middle stitch of the previous row toward the first stitch of row 2. Pick up an 11/0 (this bead is marked with a smaller dot). Continue through the cube you exited on the first stitch and the first 4 beads of the second stitch to exit the end cube (figure 1, medium blue beads and line).

8. To make the last stitch, pick up an 11/0 (dark blue with small dot), and go through the top cube on the first stitch of the previous row.

Now pick up 5 beads, starting with an 11/0. Sew through the cube you exited on the middle stitch and continue through 6 beads to exit the top cube on stitch 3 (dark blue beads and line).

9. Begin row 3 the same way you began row 2 in step 6 (figure 1, dark orange beads and line).

10. Work the second stitch like the second stitch of row 2 – step 7 (figure 1, medium orange beads and line).

11. Work the third stitch like the third stitch of the previous row – step 8 (figure 1, light orange beads and line).

12. Continue making rows until the band is the desired length.

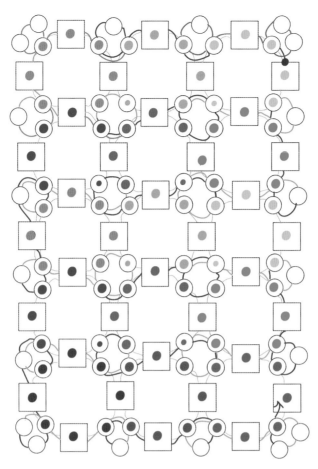

Figure 2

Second Pass and Edging

In this step, you pull the four 11/0s between the cubes into their own rings At the same time, when you reach a corner or an edge you add beads to fill in the gaps with neat, decorative triangular loops.

1. With your needle exiting a cube on one of the long edges of the last row (figure 2, green dot, top right), make a corner by going through the corner 11/0, picking up 2 11/0s, and sewing back through the corner 11/0 (figure 2, top right).

2. Work an edge stitch by continuing through the first top cube and the 2 11/0s after it. Pick up an 11/0 and sew through the original 2 11/0s in the same direction as before. Repeat with the 2 11/0s between the second and third top cubes (figure 2, green and light green lines).

3. Continue through the third top cube and the corner 11/0. Complete this corner as in step 1 by picking up 2 11/0s and sewing through the corner 11/0 again in the original direction (figure 2, top left).

4. Continue down through the first cube on the long edge and the 2 11/0s between it and the next edge cube. Add an 11/0 and sew through the first 11/0 and the horizontal cube (figure 2, upper left, orange and blue beads).

5. To work an interior ring, sew through the 2 lower 11/0s (blue), then the 2 upper 11/0s (orange) in the group. Go through the first 2 11/0s again and go through the next horizontal cube.

6. Sew around through the 2 upper then the two lower 11/0s in the next 4-bead group. Continue through the first 2 beads again and go through the last horizontal cube on the row (figure 2, orange and blue bead groups).

7. To work the first long edge stitch on the second side, sew down through the 11/0 toward the second cube on the edge. Pick up an 11/0 and sew through the 11/0 above the first one. Continue through the first 11/0 (figure 2, yellow and blue beads).

8. Work the next edge stitch by sewing through second cube and the 2 11/0s below it. Pick up an 11/0 and continue through the upper 11/0 again (figure 2, blue and yellow beads).

9. Continue through the first horizontal cube and circle around the 4 11/0s, top to bottom. Continue through the 2 top 11/0s again and go through the middle horizontal cube.

10. Circle around the next 4 11/0s, bottom to top, and continue through the bottom 2 again to go through the last horizontal cube (figure 2, blue and orange groups).

11. Work the next 2 edge stitches shown on the middle left-hand side of figure 2.

12. Continue back and forth in this manner until you have worked the other edge and corners. Then end the thread securely in the beadwork (figure 2, arrow at bottom right).

Button Closure

1. Cut a 1-yd. (.9m) thread and string an alternating pattern of 8 cubes and 8 seed beads. Sew through the 16 beads again to draw them into a tight ring. Then secure the ring with 2 surgeon's knots. Weave the thread tail back into the ring, tying a pair of half hitches between beads and going through a few more beads. Then clip it off.

2. Bring the working thread out a seed bead and string a seed, cube, seed, cube, and seed.

3. Sew through the next seed on the ring. Then sew back up the last seed and cube (photo 1).

4. String a seed, cube, and seed and sew through the next seed on the ring (photo 2). Sew back out the last seed and cube.

5. Repeat step 4 until you have sewn through the eighth seed on the ring and come back up the eighth vertical cube.

6. String a seed and sew down the first cube and the seed below it. Then go through the first seed on the ring (photo 3).

7. Come back up the first vertical seed, cube, and seed. Then sew through the remaining 7 seeds on the top. Go through all 8 top beads again to draw them into a tight ring.

8. Bring the thread out any bead on the ring and pick up a seed. Skip the next 2 seeds on the ring and sew through the next 2 (photo 4). Pick up a seed, skip 2 and go through the next 2 seeds on the ring (figure 3).

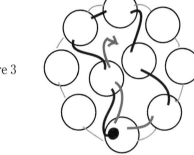

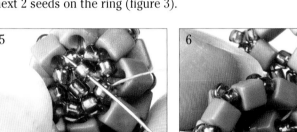

Figure 3

9. Sew through the first center seed (photo 5). Then sew through the top center of the button to the bottom.

10. To attach the button to the bracelet, string a cube and 1-2 seeds so the center stalk is a tiny bit longer than the button's height. Sew through the third horizontal cube from the end on the middle stitch.

11. String 1-2 seeds and sew back up the cube inside the button and out the center of the top (photo 6).

12. Go through the second center seed added in step 8 then the first (photo 7). Sew back down the inside cube and the first seed(s). Go through the horizontal cube on the band again. Sew back up the second seed(s) and the inside cube. Come out the top on the other side of the second center seed and go through it (photo 8).

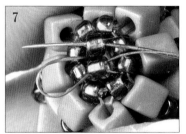

13. Sew through the other side of the first center seed so that the two center beads are joined on both sides (photo 9). If you wish, repeat the button thread path once more for additional reinforcement, ending in the same place.

14. The center beads will want to pull down into the button. To correct this problem, pick up a new seed and sew through the opposite end of the other center seed (photo 10). Go through the new bead, then the first center bead in the original direction (photo 11). Weave the thread into the button, tying several pairs of half hitches between beads before cutting off the excess.

15. Weave the starting tail through beads at the other end of the bracelet to exit the middle cube on the end. String the number of seeds you need to make a loop that will fit over the button. Then go through the middle cube from the other side. Reinforce the loop at least twice more (photo 12). Then end the thread in the bracelet as before.

Spiky Spiral Rope Earrings

Spiral rope is a wonderfully sturdy stitch that lends itself to a lot of variation by using different size and shape beads, but I find it a bit monotonous. So when I looked at it with triangle beads in mind, I got a little wild and crazy.

This version uses small beads with large holes for the core and triangles studded with spike fringe for the outside. It gains its fullness by having almost twice as many wraps as normal spiral rope. This, of course, makes it a bit time consuming, but I think the results are worth the trouble.

SUPPLIES

7-10g Japanese round seed beads, size 11/0 with <u>large</u> holes
    (11R55 opaque turquoise)
7-10g Triangle beads, size 11 (11T706 matte metallic teal iris)
2 Swarovski crystals, 8mm round (Pacific opal)
2 Swarovski crystals, 8mm flattened oval (Pacific opal)
6 Swarovski crystals, 4mm bicone (indicolite)
16 Sterling silver, square spacer beads, 2-2.5mm
20 in. (51cm) Sterling silver round wire, 22-gauge,
    dead soft or half hard
Pair of sterling silver earwires
Beading needles, size 13
Beading thread One-G, beige or light blue
Jewelry pliers (round-nose, chain-nose, flat-nose, and flush cutters)

HOW-TO

Not all size 11/0 round Japanese seed beads are equal. Some colors have smaller holes than others. Since you will be sewing through the core beads about ten times, they must have large holes. Every time you string a core bead take time to examine its hole so that you only use those with the largest holes. Note: If you wish, use size 15/0 round seeds at the end of each spike, rather than an 11/0.

If you can't live without using a particular bead color that has too-small holes, you can use Nymo O, which is extremely thin, but make sure not to use any beads with rough edges because Nymo O is not very strong.

Make the Spiky Spirals

1. String a stop bead about 12" from the end of your thread. Then string 4 seeds and 3 triangles.

2. Sew up through the 4 seeds in their original order (figure 1).

3. Sew down the first triangle. String 2 seeds. Skip the second and sew back through the first, tightening the thread so they are snug against the triangle to form a short spike fringe.

4. Sew through the second triangle, string 2 seeds for another spike fringe as in step 3.

5. Go through the third triangle and sew up the 4 seeds of the core (figure 2).

6. String 2 triangles and sew up the last 3 core seeds (figure 3).

NOTE: It is critical that each triangle wrap be made on the same side of the previous one so the wraps spiral around the core.

7. Make 1 spike fringe between the 2 triangles and sew up the 3 core seeds again (figure 4).

8. String 1 core bead and 3 triangles.

9. Sew up the last 4 core beads. Repeat steps 3-5 (figure 5).

10. String 1 core and 3 triangles. Sew up the top 4 core beads and repeat steps 3-5 (figure 6), steps 6-7 (figure 7), and steps 8-9.

11. Repeat step 10 until the spiky spiral is long enough. Notice that you repeat steps 6-7 after every second three-triangle set. My earrings have 22 core beads.

12. For subtle symmetry, when you make the spiky spiral for the second earring, position the new loops on the opposite side of the previous ones so this spiral rotates in the opposite direction.

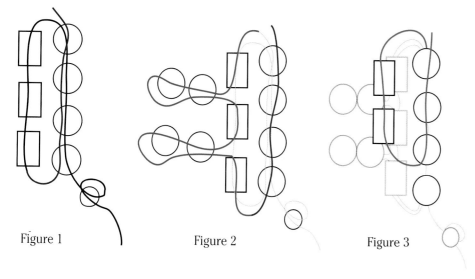

Figure 1

Figure 2

Figure 3

Make the Dangles

1. For the top dangle, cut a 2" (5cm) piece of wire and make a small wrapped loop with a single wrap at one end. String a silver spacer, an 8mm round crystal, and a silver spacer. Complete a slightly larger single-wrapped loop for the top.

2. For the dangle below the rope, cut a 2" (5cm) piece of wire and complete a small single-wrapped loop at the top end. String the 8mm flattened oval crystal and start a medium-size wrapped loop. Do not wrap yet.

3. Make 3 dangles as follows:

a. Cut a 1½" (3.8cm) piece of wire and turn a small spiral with 1½ to 2 revolutions at one end.

b. String a 4mm bicone crystal and 1 spacer bead.

c. Complete a small single-wrapped loop.

d. Repeat steps a and b but string 2 spacers, then repeat step c.

e. Repeat step d but string 3 spacers.

4. Hang the dangles in graduated order from the unwrapped loop in step 2. Then complete the wrap.

5. Repeat steps 1-4 for the other earring.

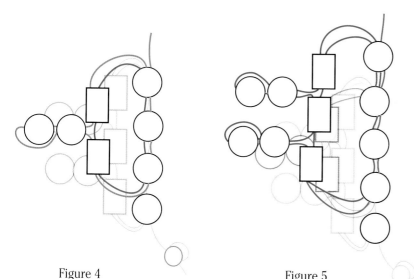

Figure 4

Figure 5

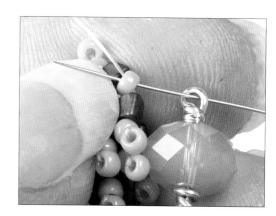

Assemble the Earrings

1. Remove the stop bead and thread a needle on the tail. Then sew the bottom of the rope to the loop above the oval crystal (photo). Sew back through the end core seed bead. Repeat this thread path at least twice more.

2. End the thread by weaving it back down through the beads on one of the triangle sets, tying two half hitches between beads at least twice. Sew through 2-3 beads before cutting the thread.

3. Sew the thread at the end of the spiral rope through the smaller loop on the round crystal as in steps 1 and 2.

4. Open the loop on an earwire sideways and hang the top loop on the round crystal from it. Close the loop securely.

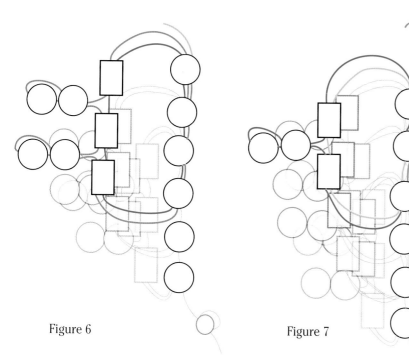

Figure 6

Figure 7

Python Necklace

I love working twisted tubular herringbone. The stitch has an almost hypnotic rhythm. It's beautiful with round beads, but triangle beads give it more texture and a sinuous feel that suggests snakeskin.

I enhanced the texture and scale-like appearance by pairing the colors in each stitch and alternating their order so that two beads of the same color are angled away from each other.

In addition to the texture and pattern of the rope, the necklace has another snaky quality. The bead at the center is built into the rope with increasing, both in stitch count and bead size, to the center then symmetrical decreasing back to the rope pattern for the second side.

I added surface embellishment to the bead to help unify the colors since the only size 5/0 triangles that I could find were a funky mint green. If you prefer to omit the embellishment, by all means, do so. In fact, you could also leave out the bead and just make a swirled "snakeskin" rope.

I've had the Scottsdale Bead Supply abalone clasp I used on the gold necklace for years; the right project never presented itself. Five closely spaced holes on each side are recessed and concealed by the top. They provide a perfect way to anchor the ends of the rope neatly and invisibly.

Supplies

20-25g Triangle beads, size 11/0, light (L) (11T262 color-lined gold/crystal AB or 11T105 transparent lime luster)
20-25g Triangle beads, size 11/0, dark (D) (11T702 matte bronze or 11T270 forest green/amber)
10g Triangle beads, size 14/0 (14T86 black/purple iris – if you can't find 14/0 triangles, use 14/0 or 15/0 round beads; 15R1829 AB green)
10g Triangle beads, size 5mm (5T952 color-lined mint green; but I recommend 507 or 508 metallic green iris, 84 metallic moss iris, or 1829 green-lined green AB if you can find one of them)
15-20g Triangle beads, size 8/0 (8T84F matte metallic moss iris)
8-10g Triangle beads, size 11/0 (11T84 metallic moss iris)
Bead thread, One-G, medium brown; green
Beading needles, size 12 or 13
Clasp with 4-5 concealed holes (Scottsdale Beading Supply); vintage glass clasp (Jess Imports)
2 Wooden beads, 10mm
1 Wooden bead, 16mm

Figure A

Ending and Adding Thread

1. You will have to end and add thread at least once. When the old thread is about 8" (20cm) long, stop after adding a pair of beads and sewing down the bead below.

2. Thread a needle with a new thread as long as you can use comfortably. Start 8-10 beads down from the top in the first column of the last stitch made (figure A, blue line at bottom). Sew up about 3 beads and tie 2 half hitches around the thread between beads.

3. Sew up 2-3 more beads and knot again. Sew up 1-2 more beads and knot a third time, then exit the top bead at the beginning of the last stitch.

4. Sew down the second bead of the stitch and the bead below it. Then sew up the top bead of the next column to begin the next stitch with the new thread (figure A, blue line at the top).

5. End the old thread with 2-3 pairs of knots between beads as you continue sewing down the column you are in (figure A, green line). End by going through a few beads. Then trim off the starting and ending tails.

New Thread   Old Thread

Modified Tubular Herringbone Start

Note: Be very careful not to split the thread.

1. String 8 size 11/0 triangle beads in the following pattern: 1L (gold), 2D (bronze), 2L, 2D, 1L and go through the first bead again (figure 1, orange line). Leave a 12" (30cm) tail for attaching the clasp.

2. For the first herringbone round:

a. Pick up 2 beads – L then D – and sew through beads #2 and 3 (2D).

b. Pick up 2 beads – D then L – and sew through beads #4 and 5 (2L).

c. Pick up 2 beads – L then D – and sew through beads #6 and 7 (2D).

d. Pick up 2 beads – D then L – and sew through beads #8 and 1 and the first bead of the first new stitch (figure 1, red line).

3. Work one more round in the established herringbone color pattern:

a. Pick up 2 beads – L then D – and sew down the dark bead on stitch #1 and up the dark bead on stitch #2.

b. Pick up 2 beads – D then L – and sew down the light bead on stitch #2 and up the light bead on stitch #3.

c. Pick up 2 beads – L then D – and sew down the dark bead on stitch #3 and up the dark bead on stitch #4.

d. Pick up 2 beads – D then L – and sew down the light bead on stitch #4 and step up through the top 2 light beads on stitch #1 (figure 1, burgundy line to first green dot, a).

stitch 2   stitch 3

c

b

1 8

d

a

e

stitch 1   Figure 1

Twisted Tubular Herringbone

Twisted tubular herringbone is usually worked with one twist stitch per round, but you can use the special stitching pattern on some or all of the stitches. In this case, I've twisted stitches #2 and #4. Note that you never sew through the size 14/0 beads on these stitches a second time.

1. Begin twisted herringbone on round 3, repeating step 3a (figure 1, green line, a-b).

2. To work a twist stitch on stitch #2, pick up 3 beads – D, 14/0, and L. Sew down 2 light beads on stitch #2. Then sew up only the top light bead of stitch #3 (photo 1 and figure 1, green line, b-c). (Note: I find that this method twists better than the method used for the other half of the rope.)

3. Work stitch #3 like step 3c (figure 1, green line, c-d).

4. Stitch #4 is a twist stitch, so pick up 3 beads – D, 14/0, and L. Sew down 2

1

light beads on stitch #4. There is no step up from now on. Instead sew up only the top light bead of stitch #1(figure 1, green line, d-e).

5. Repeat steps 1-4 around (figure 1, blue line) until the rope is about 9" (23cm) long.

Beaded Bead

Use only light beads for the first 2 increase rounds.

1. On the first increase round, add 2L to stitch #1 and go down the D on #1. Pick up 1L, then go up the D on stitch #2 (figure 2, a-b).

2. Pick up 2L and go down only the top L on stitch #2. Pick up 1L and go up the L on stitch #3 (figure 2, b-c).

3. Work stitch #3 like stitch #1, coming up the D on stitch #4 (figure 2, c-d).

4. Pick up 2L and go down only the top L on stitch #4. Pick up 1L and step up through the first bead of the previous row and the first side of stitch #1 (figure 2, d-e).

5. Work the second increase round the same way, but pick up 2 beads between stitches (figure 2, blue line). You will add 16 beads on this round. Step up as at the end of step 4 (photo 2 and figure 2, e-f).

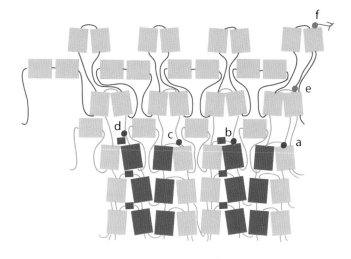

Figure 2

6. Switch to the shiny green 11/0 triangles. Work the first stitch normally and go through the first increase bead. Pick up 2 green triangles and go through the second increase bead. Then go up the first bead on stitch #2 (figure 3, a-b).

7. Work stitches #2, 3, and 4 like stitch 1. After going through the second increase bead after stitch #4 (figure 3, b-c), step up through the first 2 beads on stitch #1 for a normal step up (figure 3, c-d). You now have 8 stitches in the round and the green round has pulled the increase beads up in pairs like regular herringbone stitches. Step up normally, through 2 beads, for the rest of the beaded bead.

8. Work a second round with the green 11/0s.

9. Work 3 rounds with size 8/0 triangles.

Note: for the smaller bead on the green necklace, work a fourth round of 8/0s, putting a single 11/0 between the stitches. Omit step 10 and the repeat of step 9 in step 11. Insert only a 16mm bead. Then finish this bead with the remainder of step 11 and steps 12-14.

10. Work 1 round with size 5/0 triangles (photo 3; I didn't like the yellowish color of the 11/0 triangles I used in this photo so I pulled out the work and changed the color to dark green as described in step 6).

11. Repeat step 9 and insert a 10 and a 16mm bead. Repeat step 8, working two rounds with 11/0 green triangles. Insert the other 10mm wooden bead.

12. To decrease using all light beads, come up the first bead of the first stitch and pick up only 1 bead; go down the other bead of stitch #1 (figure 4, a-b).

13. Repeat step 12 for all 8 stitches (figure 4, b-c). Then step up through the first bead of the previous row and the first single bead (figure 4, c-d).

14. Complete the decrease on the second all light round. Pick up 2 and go through the second single bead. Go through the third single bead (figure 4, d-e), pick up 2, and go through the next 2 single beads. Repeat around, working only 4 stitches and drawing them together as you go. Step up in the normal manner (figure 4, e-f).

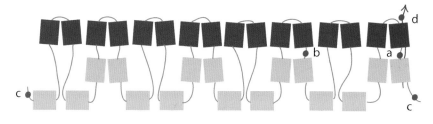

Figure 3

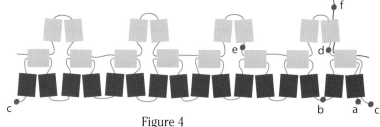

Figure 4

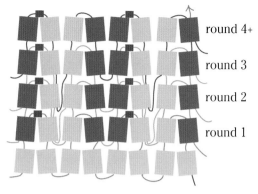

round 4+

round 3

round 2

round 1

Figure 5

Bead Embellishment

Adding surface beads over the junctions between herringbone stitches is a bit tricky because it's sometimes difficult to get the needle at the right angle, so after you've done 2-3 rows, decide whether you like the effect.

1. Start a new thread in the first side of the rope and bring the needle out the first light bead of a stitch on the last light row. Pick up an embellishment triangle and sew down the second bead of the stitch (photo 4).

Sew up the first bead of the next stitch and repeat around. End by sewing up the first light bead again. You will have placed 8 embellishment beads.

2. Continue up the first green 11/0 (photo 5).

3. Pick up an embellishment bead and go down the next green 11/0 (photo 6). Sew up the first bead of the second green stitch and repeat around.

4. On all but the first 2 embellishment rounds, you will place 16 beads. After completing the first green round, sew up the first bead of the second round, pick up an embellishment bead and go down the second bead of the first stitch as normal.

5. Then pick up an embellishment bead and sew up the first bead of the second stitch (photo 7). Repeat around, placing an embellishment bead at the top and base of each stitch. End by sewing up the first bead again and continuing up the first bead of the next round.

6. When you've added the top and base embellishment beads on the second green 11/0 round on the other side of the bead, you are finished embellishing. The top beads occupy the same position as the beads you applied on the light round.

Reverse Direction Twist

1. Establish the pattern on the first round as follows: stitch #1 – D then L; stitch #2 – L, 14/0, D; stitch #3 – D then L; stitch #4 – L, 14/0, D (figure 5, red line).

2. Begin round 2 without a step up. Add beads in the same pattern; go down 1 and up 1 on all stitches in the round (figure 5, orange line).

3. On round 3, work the first stitch as on round 2. Come up 2 beads to begin stitch #2 (figure 5, light green line), pick up the 3 beads for stitch #2 and go down 1 then up 1 for stitch #3 + 1 line.

Pick up the 2 beads for stitch #3 and go down 1 then come up 2 on stitch #4.

Pick up the 3 beads for stitch #4 and go down 1 then up 1 to begin stitch #1 again (figure 5, light green line at right).

4. Repeat step 3 until this rope is the same length as the first rope (figure 5, dark green line). End with 2 plain, untwisted rounds, omitting the 14/0s for symmetry.

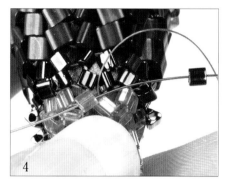

Clasp Join

1. Start by sewing 2 adjacent beads to the end hole on the clasp. Repeat the thread path twice more for security.

2. Flatten the rope and sew a bead on each side of the first attached pair to the next hole. One bead will be on the top of the flattened rope and the other will be under it. Reinforce the stitch.

3. If you clasp has five holes, skip the middle hole. Then sew the next top and bottom beads to the next hole and reinforce.

4. Finally sew the two end beads to the last hole and reinforce. Then weave the thread into the rope and end it (photo 8).

5. Pull the starting tail out of the beads you sewed into a ring and remove the ring beads until the end separates into herringbone pairs. Thread the starting tail on a needle and attach it to the other side of the clasp the same way.

6. If you're using a single-loop clasp, sew a 14/0 or 15/0 between the 4 stitch pairs as in the first decrease round (figure 4). String 3 small beads between each 15/0. Then sew the center bead of each triplet to the clasp loop.

Parquet Necklace

This bib necklace is a more complex variation on my octagon weave (see "Octagon Weave Bracelet"). Working with 4mm cube beads added a new problem: simple seed bead spacers between the cubes weren't adequate to produce a graceful shape. However, three-bead groups between each cube spaced them far enough apart to conceal the holes. The groups also increased the look of complexity by creating parallelograms between the octagons and reminded me of a favorite childhood toy, colorful parquet blocks.

To make the necklace curve gracefully, I short-

ened the spacer groups on the upper sides of the neck chain very slightly, which also meant a different edge finish on the top and bottom of the chain.

When the beading was finished, I decided that the necklace needed something more, so I added a crystal checkerboard on the front and carried the crystals up every other octagon on the chain. The necklace looks difficult because of the variety of geometrical shapes – octagons, parallelograms, and triangles – but worked step-by-step, it's almost as easy as the "Octagon Weave Bracelet."

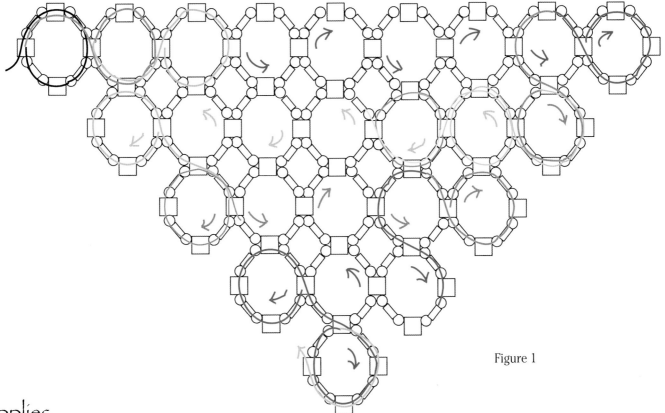

Figure 1

Supplies

30g Cube beads, 4mm (4C707 metallic matte green)
15g Triangle beads, size 11/0 (11T84 metallic green luster)
10g Round seed beads, size 11/0 (11R180 green AB)
31-35 Swarovski crystals, round, 6mm (shadow)
10 Swarovski crystals, round, 6mm (tourmaline)
Beading thread, One-G, dark green and pale gray or white
Beading needles, size 10
Vermeil hook clasp (Fire Mountain Gems)

The Bib Octagons

1. Figure 1 shows the entire bib portion of the necklace; it starts at the top left. Start with a 2- to 3-yd. (1.8-2.7m) single thread and pick up the following pattern: cube, group (seed, triangle, seed), cube, group, cube, group, cube, and group. Leaving a 4" (10cm) tail to weave in later, tie the beads into a snug ring and pass the needle through the first 2 cubes and groups to exit the third cube (figure 1, black to orange line).

2. For the second stitch pick up a group, cube, group, cube, group, cube, and group and go through the cube you exited on the first stitch in the same direction (toward the thread) to make a second ring attached to the first. Continue through the next 2 groups and cubes to exit the end cube (figure 1, orange to yellow line).

3. Make a total of 9 stitches for the first row. The arrows on the row show the stitching direction. Notice that you reverse direction with every stitch, as you do in right-angle weave.

4. After completing the ninth stitch and going through the cube that connects it to the eighth stitch, continue around the top of the eighth stitch toward the seventh, exiting the bottom cube (figure 1, orange line on right).

5. For the first stitch on row 2, pick up a group, cube, group, cube, group, cube, and group. Sew through the bottom cube on stitch 8 of row 1 and continue around the beads of the first row 2 stitch to exit the third cube (figure 1, orange to yellow line).

6. To begin the second stitch, pick up a group and go through the bottom cube on stitch 7 of row 1 (figure 1, yellow line). Pick up, a group, cube, group, cube, and group. Go through the side cube of the previous row 2 stitch. Continue around the new stitch to exit the cube on the other side (figure 1, light green line).

7. For stitch 3, pick up a group, cube, group, cube, and group. Then go through the bottom cube on the sixth stitch of row 1 toward the seventh stitch (figure 1, green line). Pick up a group and sew down through the cube between this and the previous row 2 stitch (figure 1, orange line).

Continue around the bottom of the last stitch to exit the side cube (figure 1, bright yellow line).

8. For stitch 4, repeat the pattern of step 6, going through the bottom cube on stitch 5 of row 1.

9. Repeat step 7 for stitch 5, step 6 for stitch 6, and step 7 for stitch 7.

10. To step down and begin row 3 when you've completed the seventh stitch of row 2 and gone through the cube between stitches 6 and 7, continue around the lower left of stitch 6, exiting its bottom cube figure 1, yellow line at left).

11. Pick up 4 groups and 3 cubes for the first row 3 stitch and continue around it to exit the first cube on the inner side (figure 1, yellow to orange line).

12. Repeat steps 7, 6, 7, and 6 to complete the 5 stitches of row 3.

13. Step down and begin row 4 by repeating steps 4 and 5 (figure 1, orange to red line on right).

14. Repeat steps 6 and 7 to complete the other 2 stitches of row 4.

15. Step down to work the single stitch of row 5 the same way you began row 3 in steps 10 and 11. End coming out the left side cube (figure 1, red to yellow line).

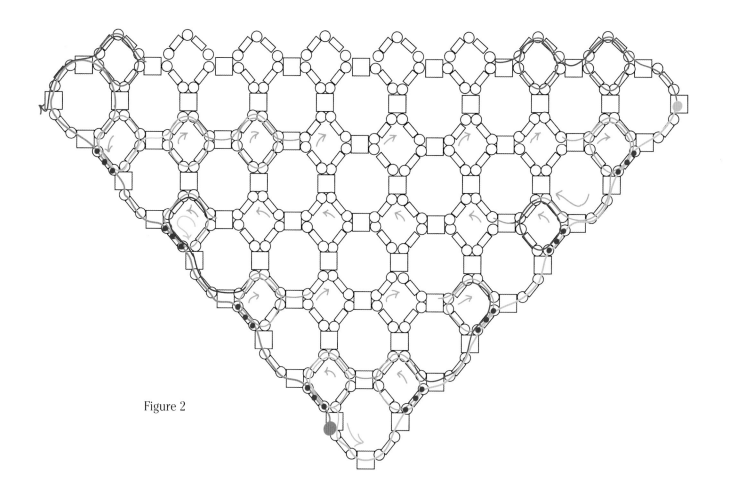

Figure 2

The Bib Parallelograms

1. The first step in drawing the 3-bead groups together to form parallelograms is to add groups that close the left side of the bib (see figure 2, orange line and dark green dotted beads). Exiting the left side of the bottom stitch (figure 2, large orange dot), pick up a 3-bead group.

2. Sew right to left through the bottom cube of the edge stitch on row 4 and continue around the left side of the stitch to exit the side cube. Pick up a new 3-bead group.

3. Repeat step 2 twice more and end by going around the left-most stitch of row 1 exiting the group before the bottom cube (figure 2, orange line at top left).

4. Sew counterclockwise through the 4 adjacent groups between rows 1 and 2 to pull them together and continue through the bottom cube of the second row 1 stitch (figure 2, medium to yellow-green line).

5. Sew clockwise through the next square of 4 groups and continue around to pass through the bottom cube of stitch 3 (figure 2, light green to gray line). Repeat this pattern to pull all but the last set of groups together between rows 1 and 2.

6. To complete the rightmost parallelogram between the first 2 rows, sew clockwise through the 2 upper groups. Pick up 3 beads to make the group on the lower right-hand side and complete the parallelogram by sewing through the group on the top right of the first stitch of row 2. Continue through the first 3 groups again and go down the side cube of row 2 then the outer side and bottom cube of the first row 2 stitch (figure 2, top right dotted green beads and green line).

7. For the first parallelogram between rows 2 and 3, go counterclockwise through the 3 groups on the edge (figure 2, green to blue line). Pick up the 3 beads for the fourth side and continue through the top 2 groups again then the bottom cube of the second stitch on row 2 (figure 2, blue to gray line and dotted green beads).

8. Work counterclockwise to pull the remaining 5 parallelograms together. Follow the blue line on the left side through the top and side of the last parallelogram again (figure 2) to step down to the next row of parallelograms.

9. Work clockwise to pull the parallelograms between rows 3 and 4 together. You'll need to add the side group on the rightmost stitch and step down to the last row as you did in steps 6-7 (figure 2, green to blue line on right).

10. After joining the second parallelogram, continue around the left side of the parallelogram and the side and bottom of the bottom octagon (figure 2, green to yellow line).

11. To even the outer right-hand edge of the bib, follow the yellow line through the edge cubes and groups to the edge cube of row 1 (figure 2, large yellow dot), and weave the thread into the bead-work to end it.

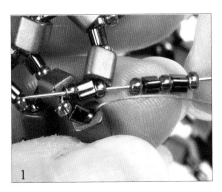

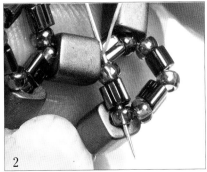

Bib Top Edge

1. Weave a new 2- to 3-yd. (1.8-2.7m) thread into the beadwork so that it exits the rightmost cube of row 1, pointing toward the top of the row. Go through the outside group and top cube (figure 2, yellow dot to red line).

2. Pick up a seed, triangle, seed, triangle, and seed and sew through the 2 top groups between octagons 8 and 9 from left to right (figure 2, red line and photos 1 and 2).

Go through the 5 new beads again (figure 2, blue line and photo 3).

3. Continue through the top cube of the eighth stitch (photo 4 and figure 2, blue line).

4. Repeat from step 2 until you've added 8 peaks across the top of the bib. End by going through the last set of 5 beads again and continue through the top and left-hand side of the first stitch (figure 2, blue line on left). You are now in position to begin the neck chain on the left side.

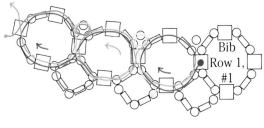

Figure 3

Neck Chain

1. Your needle is coming out the edge cube of the bib toward the bottom edge of the chain. Therefore string a group, cube, group, and cube. For the top side of the first chain stitch, string a seed, tri-angle, cube, triangle, and seed (the top groups are both short a seed). Then pass the needle through the edge cube in the original direction (down) to pull the first stitch into a ring (figure 3, blue to green line on right and photo 5).

continued on page 24

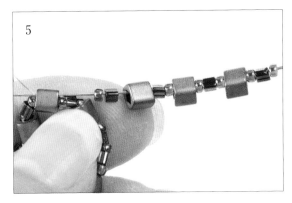

Neck Chain, continued from page 23

2. Continue through the beads on the bottom of the stitch to exit the end cube (figure 3, green line and photo 6).

3. With your needle pointing toward the top of the chain, string a seed, triangle, cube, triangle, and seed. Then string a cube, group, cube, and group for the bottom of the second stitch and go up through the cube from which you started (figure 3, green to blue line and photo 7).

4. Continue through the beads on the top of the stitch to exit the end cube.

5. Alternate steps 1 and 2 then 3 and 4 until this half of the neck chain has an odd number of stitches and is the desired length minus the clasp. (I have 17 stitches on the clasp ring side of my chain.)

6. With the needle exiting the end cube and pointing up, string 3 seeds, the ring part of the clasp and 5 seeds. Sew down the third seed toward the cube (photo 8).

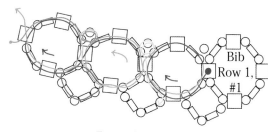

Figure 3

7. String 2 seeds and sew through the end cube toward the first 3 seeds (photo 9). Reinforce the clasp attachment with 2-3 more thread passes.

8. Continue up through the end cube, and the 5 beads on the top of the end stitch (figure 3, orange dot and line on left). Then sew through the seed bead at the beginning of the top of the next stitch (photo 10).

9. Pick up 1 seed and sew through the pair of seeds between stitches (photo 11 and figure 3, orange line).

10. Sew through the new seed and the first of the 2 seeds again. Then sew down the cube between the stitches and through the group on the second stitch (toward the bib) – (photo 12 and figure 3, orange to yellow line).

11. Pick up a seed, triangle, seed, triangle, and seed and sew through the bottom group on the end stitch (photo 13 and figure 3, yellow to red line).

12. Continue through the group on the second stitch (photo 14 and figure 3, red line continued).

13. Then sew through the bottom cube and the second group on the second stitch, the side cube, and the seed above it on the third stitch (photo 15 and figure 3, red to light orange line).

14. Repeat from step 9 (figure 3, bright yellow line) until you have embellished both edges of the chain back to the bib. End the thread securely in the beadwork.

15. Weave in a new thread positioned so it is coming up out of the end cube at the other edge of row 1. You'll start the first chain stitch picking up the beads for the top side. Work an even number of stitches that is one less than you worked on the first side (I have 16). Your needle will be positioned identically to the way it was when you added the clasp ring – coming up out of the end cube. Add the hook part of the clasp the same way (steps 6 and 7). Then embellish both sides of the chain back to the bib (steps 8 - 14) and end the thread.

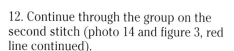
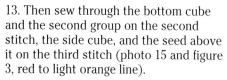
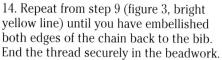

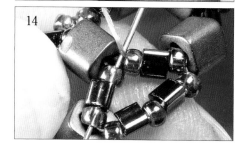
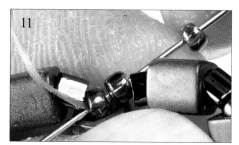

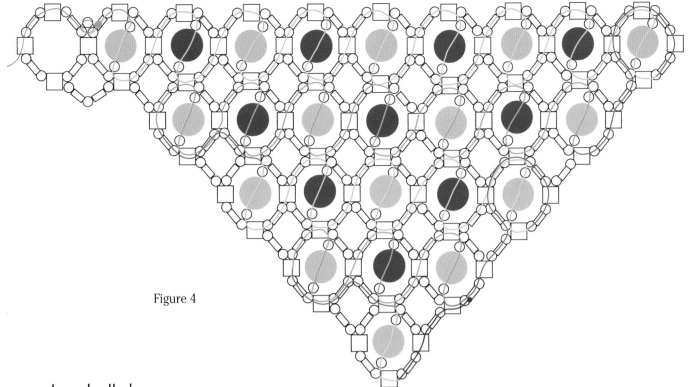

Figure 4

Crystal Embellishment

If you're happy with your necklace, stop here, or continue for some bling.

1. Work with a long doubled thread – about 2½ to 3 yd. (2.3-2.7m). When tightening a crystal in position, be careful to pull the thread straight through the crystal. Do not pull it up against the edge of the crystal, or the thread is likely to be cut.

2. Anchor the thread securely in the last stitch on the ring end of the chain (the odd-numbered side). Then weave around the stitch to exit the top cube of the next chain stitch with the needle pointing toward the bib.

3. Pick up a seed, a light crystal, and a seed and sew through the bottom cube of the same stitch toward the bib (photo 16).

4. Work up the side between the second and third stitches, over the top of the third stitch and around the 3 seeds between the third and fourth stitches. Continue through the top of the fourth stitch to exit the top cube, pointing toward the bib(figure 4, top left). Add a seed, light crystal, and seed in the same manner.

5. Continue placing light crystals over every even numbered stitch on the chain. The chain stitch closest to the bib will not have a crystal (figure 4, top left to orange dot).

6. On the bib, you'll place a crystal over every stitch. For the first row, alternate light and dark crystals, beginning and ending with a light crystal (photo 17 and figure 4, from the orange dot at left, yellow line).

7. Needle down to the second row by backtracking through the last stitch of row 1 and the parallelogram on the outer edge(figure 4, red line on right) so your needle is coming out the bottom cube in the correct direction.

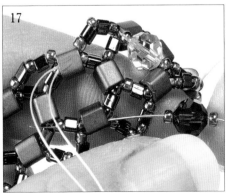

8. Place 7 crystals on row 2 beginning and ending with a light crystal (figure 4, orange line from right to left).

9. Follow the red line on the left around the bottom of the last 2 stitches of row 2, and through the top cube of the first row 3 stitch to position your needle correctly (figure 4, red line on left). Place 5 crystals, beginning and ending with a light crystal (yellow line from left to right).

10. Repeat step 7 to reposition your needle (figure 4, red line at middle right) and place 3 crystals on row 4 (figure 4, orange line). Reposition your needle as in step 9 (figure 4, red line on bottom left) and set one light crystal on row 5 (figure 4, yellow line).

11. If at least 40" (1m) of thread remains, work through the bib edge (figure 4, burgundy line and dot) to come out the top cube on the second stitch on the hook side of the chain, pointing toward the hook, and place light crystals on every other stitch. There will be a crystal on the last stitch. End the thread securely in the beadwork.

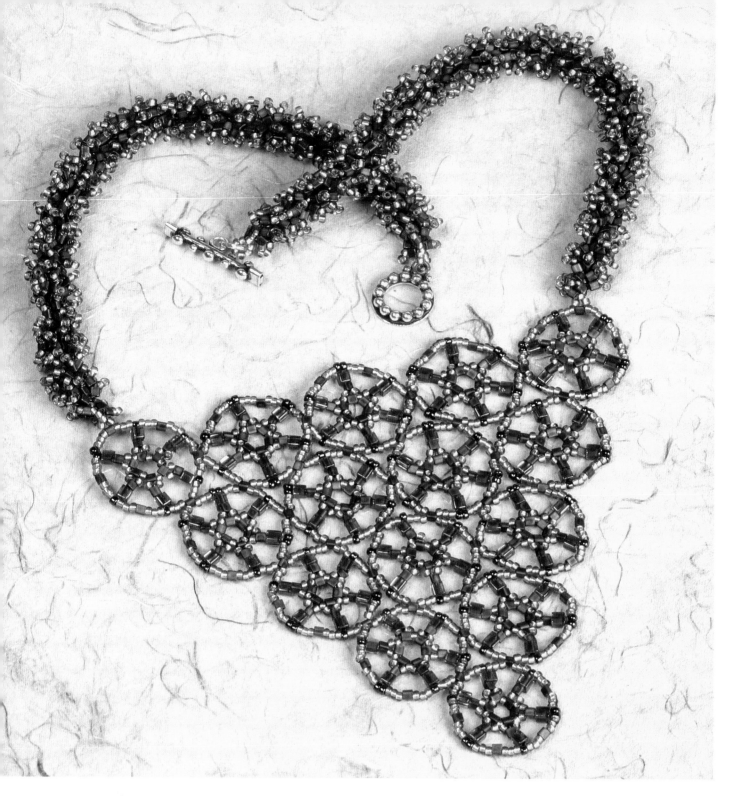

Wheels within Wheels Necklace

Make a bib of linked hexagons and add a spiky spiral rope neck chain.

About a year ago a dear friend asked me to figure out how to work a linked hexagon pattern. She'd taken a class and had been thoroughly confused, then left at sea because there was no handout. At the time, I made a terrible sketch that didn't help her much, and from time to time,

she asked if I had solved her problem yet.

Finally, I decided to take action and figure out a logical way of doing this complex-looking construction. The bib was so pretty when I'd finished it that I had to invent a special neck chain to complement it.

You'll find the directions for my lushly fringed spiral rope in "Spiky Spiral Rope Earrings."

Supplies

30-40g Size 11/0 triangle beads (11T86F, matte purple/teal/bronze rainbow)
20-30g Size 11/0 seed beads, color A (11R39F, matte silver-lined lavender)
2-3g Size 11/0 seed beads, color B (11R504, metallic purple luster)
20g Cube beads, 3mm (3C1058, purple-lined clear)
Sterling silver toggle clasp with beaded design (BeadBabe.com, #SB-003)
Beading needles, size 13 for rope and size 10 for bib
Beading thread, One-G, purple

First Hexagon Wheel

1. To make the bib, start with the bottom-most hexagon (wheel). Start with a single 2-3-yd. (1.8-2.7m) thread and a size 10 needle.

2. For the first wheel, string the beads for the center circle first. Alternate 1 color A seed with 1 triangle 6 times. Leaving a 4-6" (10-15cm) thread tail, tie the beads into a ring with a surgeon's knot (figure 1, burgundy dot and line).

3. Sew through the first seed and the first triangle, then string the beads for the first side of the first spoke (labeled 1): 1A, triangle, and cube.

4. Working around the hexagon in a counterclockwise direction, string 3A, 1 triangle, 3A, cube, triangle, and 1A. Then sew right to left through the sixth triangle of the center circle and string 1A (figure 1, red to yellow line).

Sew back through the last triangle and cube (spoke #2).

5. Repeat step 4 four more times to make spokes #3-6 (figure 1, orange, yellow, light green, and green to teal lines).

6. With your needle exiting the sixth cube, string 3A, 1 triangle, and 3A. Sew down the cube and triangle of the first spoke and string 1A. Go through the first triangle on the circle again from left to right (figure 1, teal line).

7. Sew back up the first A and the triangle and cube of spoke #1 and go through the 7 outer edge beads between spokes #1 and #2 (figure 1, teal to light blue line).

8. String 1 or 2 color B seeds (the number will vary occasionally in order to make the hexagon lie flat). Go through the next 7 edge beads and repeat this step around the ring until you've placed 1-2B beads over each cube (figure 1, light blue line).

9. End the first ring by going through the first 4 edge beads again and exiting the triangle between spokes #1 and #2 (figure 1, dark blue line).

Hexagon Row 2

The second row of the bib has 2 hexagons. Each of these shares one edge triangle with the first hexagon and the 2 hexagons on the row also share an edge triangle.

1. With your needle exiting the shared triangle from hexagon A (figure 2, red line), string 3A beads, a cube, triangle, and 1A for the first side of spoke #1 on hexagon B. Then string the beads for the center circle starting with a triangle and alternating 6 triangles and 6A beads (figure 2, red line).

2. Continue through the first triangle strung for the center and string 1A. Then go back up the triangle and cube of spoke #1 (figure 2, red to orange line).

3. Repeat step 4 of the first hexagon, but this time sew around the new hexagon in a clockwise direction and go left to right through the triangles on the center circle (figure 2, orange to light blue line).

continued on page 28

How-to

When you have to end and add thread, do so in the center ring of a hexagon where the half hitches will cause the least problem. Then come out the last spoke worked to resume beading.

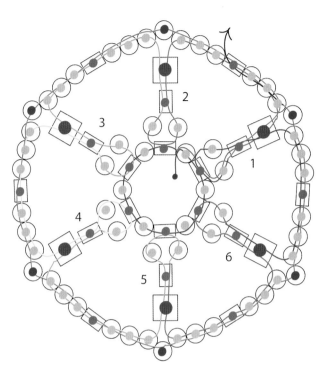

Figure 1

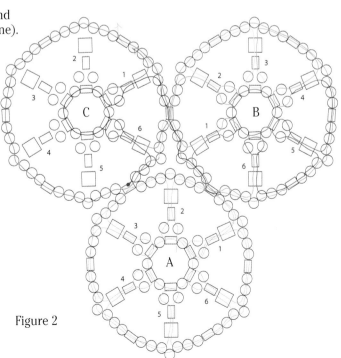

Figure 2

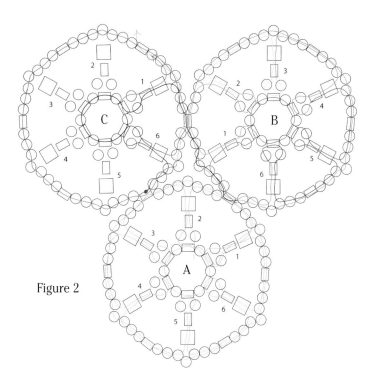

Figure 2

Hexagon Row 2, continued from page 27

4. After completing spoke 6, string 3A and go through the shared triangle again. String 3A then 1B and continue all the way around the outer edge, placing 1-2B beads over the cubes (figure 2, light blue line).

5. End hexagon B by going through the shared triangle, the 7 edge seed beads, and the triangle between spokes #1 and #2. This triangle will be shared with hexagon C (figure 2, dark blue line).

6. Work hexagon C by repeating steps 1-4. This time you will be working in a counterclockwise direction (figure 2, dark blue to red line). After stringing the 3A beads that follow spoke #5, go through the edge triangle on hexagon A between spokes #3 and #2 (figure 2, dark green dot).

7. String the 3A after the shared triangle, then work spoke #6 (figure 2, dark green line).

End with 3A. Then continue around all the beads on the outer edge, adding 1-2B above each cube (figure 2, medium green line).

8. After adding the B bead above spoke #6, continue through the edge of hexagon C to exit the triangle between spokes #1 and #2 (figure 2, yellow-green line).

Hexagon Rows 3 and 4

Figure 3 is a schematic drawing of the way the four rows of hexagons fit together. Shared triangles are colored red. Blue triangles are not shared, and the purple triangles on the top outside corners are where the neck chain attaches. The yellow arrows indicate the transition points between the hexagons and show the sewing direction. The hexagons are worked in alphabetical order, and the spokes of each hexagon are indicated by thick black lines and numbered according to their working order.

1. Begin row 3 by exiting the triangle between spokes #1 and #2 of hexagon C. This triangle will be shared between spokes #6 and #1 of hexagon D, the middle wheel on row 3. Work around it in a clockwise direction. After working spoke #5, share the triangle between spokes #3 and #2 of hexagon B.

2. Come out the triangle between spokes #1 and #2 on hexagon D to begin hexagon E, to D's left, and work around it in a counterclockwise direction. After working spoke #5, share the triangle between spokes #3 and #2 on hexagon C.

3. After completing hexagon E, go through the triangle it shares with D and follow the edge beads on D around the top, coming out the triangle after spoke #4, which D shares with F. Work counterclockwise around F. Share the triangle on B between spokes #3 and #4 on F between spokes #1 and #2.

4. To begin row 4 with hexagon G, go around the bottom and right-hand edge of F to exit the shared triangle on F between spokes #4 and #5. Work around G clockwise. You may want to sew around its edge an extra time to reinforce it since the chain attaches between spokes #3 and #4.

5. Exit and share the triangle on G between spokes #1 and #2 with H. Work around it counterclockwise. After working spoke #4, share the triangle on D

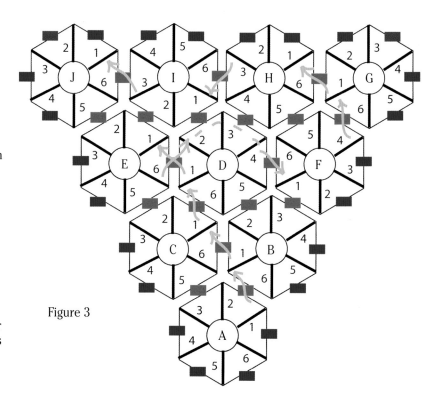

Figure 3

between its spokes #3 and #4. Work spoke #5 on H, then share the triangle between spokes #6 and #5 on F.

6. Finish H and continue around its top to exit and share its triangle between spokes #3 and #4 with hexagon I. Work around I in a clockwise direction. After working spoke #1, share the triangle on D between spokes #2 and #3. Work the second spoke on I then share the triangle on E between spokes #1 and #2.

7. Complete hexagon I and continue around its bottom edge to exit the triangle between spokes #3 and #4, which is shared with hexagon J. Work counterclockwise around J, and after working spoke #5, share the triangle on E between spokes #3 and #2. If possible, go around J an extra time to reinforce its edge, as you did with G.

Spiky Spiral Rope Chain

I worked two 6½" (16.4cm) lengths of spiky spiral rope for the sides of the necklace, spiraling them in opposite directions. See "Spiky Spiral Rope Earrings" for directions. Leave 8" (20cm) starting thread tails.

1. Thread a needle on the starting tail of one chain piece. String 7A beads and go through the loop on one of the clasp parts. Then sew back through the first A toward the rope, being careful not to split the thread (photo 1).

2. Tighten the beads up to the chain. and sew into the first core A of the chain (photo 2).

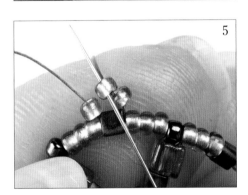

3. Sew through the beads of the first spike and back out the triangle of the spike. Then go back through the first A of step 1 toward the loop (photo 3).

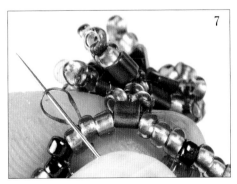

4. Reinforce the loop by repeating the thread path established in steps 1-3 as many times as possible. Then end the thread in the spike with 2 pairs of half hitches between beads (photo 4).

5. Repeat steps 1-4 to attach the other clasp part to the starting tail on the other chain piece.

6. With a needle on the thread at the final end of one of the spiral ropes, string 2A beads and sew through one of the purple-marked triangles in figure 3. String 1A, then sew back through the first of the 2A toward the rope (photo 5). Tighten the thread to pull the spiral rope against the corner hexagon.

7. Sew back into the last spike on the rope as you did with the clasp attachment (photo 6). Then repeat the joining thread path 2-3 times to reinforce it.

8. End with the needle going through a few beads on the hexagon edge and tie 2-3 pairs of half hitches between beads (photo 7). Go through a few beads before clipping off the excess thread.

9. Repeat steps 6-8 to join the other spiral rope to the other purple-marked triangle bead.

Saturn Bracelet

Turn heads with a wearable art bracelet. I must confess that this double-layer bracelet was originally intended to be a single-layer collar, but the beads had something else in mind. As I'm sure you're aware, acquiring a wide range of coordinating colors in cube and triangle sizes ranging from 2mm and 14/0 to 4mm and 5/0 is not the easiest thing in the world. Fortunately, I had some sample packs of the smaller and larger beads, but the quantities were limited – I didn't have enough for a collar. I also discovered that starting with very tiny beads on the inner edge results in too tight a curve for a necklace.

So there I was with a wonderful disc of graduated beads that could never in a million years be a necklace. The answer was obvious: make a

bracelet. But a single layer of wide, flat herringbone couldn't possibly stand up around my wrist. It would look floppy and stupid. Voilà! Make it a double layer filled with a padded stiff form.

This project offers a number of challenges, particularly beginning the second layer off the end of the first layer on the other side of the clasp and sharing beads on the edges of the first layer. It is difficult to put on and take off without help since you have to flex the inner form to twist the edge of the clasp into position to meet itself. And it's definitely not for everyday; a stand-out disc makes working at a keyboard nearly impossible.

But if you want to be noticed at a gallery opening or an evening party, it's just the ticket.

SUPPLIES

Color Key

- ● A 15R
- ■ B 14T
- ● C 11R
- ● D 8R
- ■ E 2C
- ■ F 11T
- ■ G 3C
- ■ H 8T
- ■ J 4C
- ● K 8R

5-7g Seed beads, size 15/0 (15R505 metallic blue/purple) – color A
5g Triangle beads, size 14/0 (14T85 metallic purple/bronze) – color B
10-12g Seed beads, size 11/0 (11R85 metallic purple/bronze) – color C
7-10g Seed beads, size 8/0 (8R2124 silver-lined light purple raku) – color D
7-10g Cube beads, 2mm (2C1204 marbled light purple) – color E
10g Triangle beads, size 11/0 (11T82F matte metallic blue iris) – color F
25-30g Cube beads, 3mm (3C705 matte metallic blue/purple) – color G
25-30g Triangle beads, size 8/0 (8T82 metallic blue iris) – color H
25-30g Cube beads, 4mm (4C932 blue-lined bright blue) – color J
7-10g Seed beads, size 8/0 (8R82F matte metallic blue iris) – color K
Clasp, sterling silver, 5-hole slide
Beading thread, One-G, dark blue
Beading needles, sizes 12 and 13
Plastic gallon milk jug
Permanent marker
Polyfil quilt batting
Barge cement • White glue

How-To

Work the herringbone widthwise, starting with a true herringbone start. For the first layer, continue around in pattern until the ends almost meet, leaving room for the slider clasp. Construct the double-layer, padded plastic insert. While it is curing, attach the final end to one of the clasp parts. Then begin the second layer coming out the holes of the clasp. As you work layer two, share edge beads from layer one on both inner and outer edges. When layer two is about half finished, carefully insert the plastic form, then finish the layer. Finally join both layers and the second clasp part, then edge the outside.

Figure 1

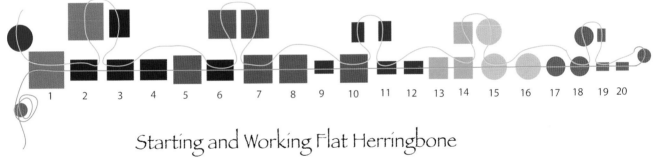

1 2 3 4 5 6 7 8 9 10 11 12 13 14 15 16 17 18 19 20

Starting and Working Flat Herringbone

Refer to "Python Necklace" (figure A) for directions on ending and adding thread. The beads are labeled A-K in the supply list. Remember to nudge them into position side by side as you work the herringbone.

1. Thread a needle with as long a single thread as is comfortable. Leave a 6" (15cm) tail and string a temporary stop bead, going through it twice so it will be secure (be careful not to split the thread). Note: beads A and K (see the key) are turn beads and do not count in the column and bead numbering of the rows.

2. String the first 2 rows starting at the outer edge as follows:

1J, 3H, 1G, 1H, 2G, 1F, 1G, 2F, 2E, 2D, 2C, 2B, 1A (turn bead) (figure 1, orange line and numbered beads).

3. The beads will twist and behave very badly as you pull them into a herringbone configuration with row 3. After you've completed row 4, they will become completely manageable. Be extremely careful not to split the thread; if you do, you'll have to start over. For row 3:

a. Sew through bead #19, the first B. Pick up 1B and 1C and sew through bead #18, the second C strung.

b. Skip beads #17 and 16 (C and D) and go through bead #15 (D). Pick up 1D and 1E and sew through bead #14, the

second E strung.

c. Skip beads #13 and 12 and sew through #11, the first of the pair of Fs. Pick up 2F and sew through bead #10 (G).

d. Skip #9 and 8, an F and a G, and sew through #7, the first of the pair of Gs. String 2G and sew through #6, the single H.

e. Skip #5 and 4, a G and an H, and sew through #3, the middle H in the group of 3. Pick up an H and a J, and sew through beads #2 and 1, an H then a J.

f. Pick up a K for a turn bead. (figure 1, yellow line).

1

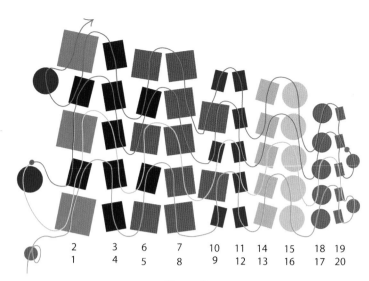

Figure 2

| 2 | | 3 | 6 | | 7 | | 10 | 11 | 14 | | 15 | | 18 | 19 |
| 1 | | 4 | 5 | | 8 | | 9 | 12 | 13 | | 16 | | 17 | 20 |

●	A 15R
■	B 14T
●	C 11R
●	D 8R
■	E 2C
■	F 11T
■	G 3C
■	H 8T
■	J 4C
●	K 8R

c. Pick up a G and an F and sew down the first F of the third pair then up the E of the second pair.

d. Pick up an E and a D and sew down the D of the pair then up the C of the first pair.

e. Pick up a C and a B and sew down the B of the first pair.

f. Pick up an A for the turn on the inner edge and sew back up the last B added to step up (figure 2, red dot and line to green dot and beginning of green line).

6. Row 5 is also shown in figure 2 with the green line. Notice that you add turn beads on the inner edge at the end of even-numbered rows and on the outer edge at the end of odd-numbered rows. Complete each turn by sewing through the last bead added.

7. Work in the pattern established until the ends of the piece almost meet. Leave a space the width of the clasp.

8. When you've added the last row of beads, an odd-numbered row, add a K turn bead and sew down then up the top row of beads to tighten the edge. Then sew back through the last row (photo 1) so you are exiting the J and pointing away from the beadwork. Leave the working thread in place if it's at least 24" (61cm) long. If not, end it securely.

Starting and Working Flat Herringbone, continued from page 31

4. Tighten both the working thread and the stop bead to draw the beads together into 10 columns, each 3 beads tall (figure 2, orange and yellow lines at bottom). Hold the twisty mess pinched between your thumb and index finger with the added beads (row 3) on top. The next row will make all secure.

5. To begin row 4, sew up the edge H (bead #2) and the J you just added.

a. Pick up 2H and sew down the H you added in the last pair. Then sew up the second G added in the next-to-last pair.

b. Pick up an H and a G and sew down the first G of the pair then up the second F in the third pair.

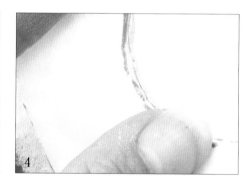

Making the Stiff Liner

1. Cut two flat sides from a plastic gallon milk jug. Lay the bracelet on one of the pieces of plastic and use a permanent marker to dot the inner and outer edges (photo 2).

2. Cut out the first piece and trim it to be about ⅛" (3mm) smaller than the beadwork on the inner, outer and straight edges. When the first piece is the right size, cut the second to match.

3. Open the polyfil quilt batting to a single layer and cut two rings whose outer edges match the outside edge of the plastic. The inside edges should be about half the width of the plastic and the straight edges should be a bit shy of the straight edges of the plastic.

4. Glue each batting ring to a plastic ring using Barge cement or E6000 (photo 3).

5. When the glue is dry, glue the batted sides of the two plastic rings together, taking care to join the plastic inner and straight edges (photo 4).

6. Wisps of batting sticking out the edge of your bracelet will ruin the effect, so when the Barge cement is dry, spread white glue generously along the batting edge of the form to seal it completely. I used my finger to spread the glue over the batting and push the batting down into the edge of the plastic. It's a messy job, but white glue will wash off with soap and water. Lay the piece aside to dry completely.

7. If, when you are ready to insert the form, it's a bit too wide to fit inside the double layer of beads, use sharp utility scissors or tin snips to trim it a bit more as needed. You should have used so much white glue that trimming will not expose wisps; if not, touch up the white glue and let it dry completely again.

Joining the First Clasp Part

1. Make sure the clasp will open outward. With the working thread (or a new thread) exiting the end bead (J), sew the first two end beads to the end and second loops of the clasp in a reinforced figure-8 pattern (photo).

2. Repeat the reinforced figure-8 pattern to attach the next 2 edge beads to the second and third clasp loops (photo 6).

3. Sew the 2 beads of the third stitch to the fourth loop and the two beads of the fourth stitch to the inner loop, reinforcing both joins. Don't worry about the fifth stitch.

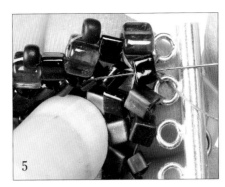

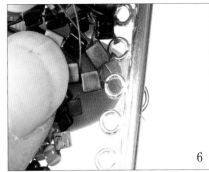

Figure 3

Starting the Second Layer

On figure 3, the beads of the first layer, including the shared edge beads, are shaded lighter than the beads of the second layer. The pairs slant in opposite directions on the two layers.

1. To start layer 2 attached to the clasp (figure 3, orange line), work back to the outer edge. Sew through the end clasp loop to the side opposite layer 1. String 1J and 1H and sew down the second clasp loop toward layer 1 (photo 7). On layer 1, sew through the second bead from the end (H), then down the third bead G) toward the clasp and come through the third loop to the new side.

2. Pick up 2G and sew back through the same clasp loop to layer 1 (photo 8). Sew away from the clasp through the fourth bead, then toward the clasp through the fifth bead (G and F).

3. Come through the fourth loop (photo 9). Pick up 2F and sew back through the fourth loop (photo 10). Sew away from the clasp through the sixth bead (F), then back toward the clasp through the seventh bead (E).

4. Come through the fifth loop and pick up 1E and 1D. Sew back through the loop (photo 11).

5. Pick up 1C and sew down the end B toward the clasp on the finished side (photo 12).

6. Sew up the A and the second B (photo 13 and figure 3, orange to green line). Note: on the inner edge, you'll share the Bs and the A turn beads on the first side with the second side – except for the second time you come to the inner edge (step 14).

7. Pick up 1C and sew down the new C from step 5, then up the new D from step 4 (photo 14).

8. Pick up 1D and 1E, sew down the first E from step 4 and up the near F from step 3.

9. Pick up an F and a G and sew down the next F from step 3, then up the near G from step 2.

10. Pick up a G and an H and sew down the next G from step 2 and up the H from step 1.

11. Pick up 2H and sew down the new J from step 1.

12. Pick up a K turn bead and sew through the last H added (photo 15 and figure 3, green line).

13. Work a row of herringbone following the pattern for row 3 (see figure 2) in the opposite direction – from big to small beads. After adding the E and D, go down the previous D and up the previous C.

continued on page 34

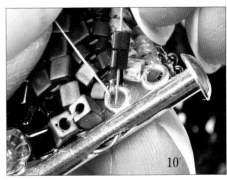

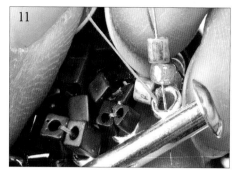

Starting the Second Layer, continued from page 33

14. Pick up the third C and sew down the second B on the first side (figure 3, red line). Pick up an A turn bead and sew up the third B on side #1 (photo 16). Pick up the fourth C (figure 3, red to yellow line).

15. Sew down the previous (third) C added in step 14, then up the D added in step 13.

16. Work a row of herringbone following the pattern for row 4 (see figure 2) but working in the opposite direction – from small to big beads – until you've added the final pair of Hs and gone down the J from the previous row. Go through the K turn bead on side 1 and come back up the last H added (photo 17 and figure 3, yellow line). The shared bead on this edge is the K turn bead from now on.

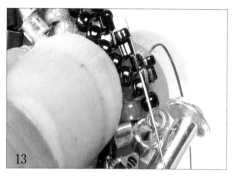

17. Work row 5 of herringbone following the pattern for row 3 (figure 3, orange line). After adding the E and D, go down the previous D and up the fourth C. Pick up the fifth C and sew down the fourth B and up the second A on the first side. Sew up the fifth B and pick up the sixth C (figure 3, orange to dark red line).

18. Repeat from step 15 (figure 3, dark red line) until you've completed about half the second side.

19. Carefully insert the stiffener between the layers, wiggling and pushing it in until it reaches the clasp (photo 18). It should be snug but if the fit is too tight, trim it slightly.

20. Finish the second side so that the straight edges of both sides are even and slightly overlap the stiffener. End with a row 3 pattern, then sew back to the large bead end, going up and down the last row of beads to pull the edge together as in step 7 (photo 1) of "Starting and working flat herringbone."

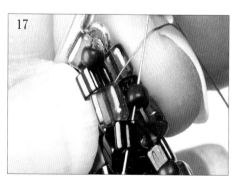

row 1, side 1

last row, side 2

Figure 4

Joining the Ends

Sew the second clasp part to the end of the bracelet as you join the ends (figure 4). This process is a bit fiddly, and you might find that a slightly different stitching path looks neater on your bracelet. Take time to evaluate the look of every stitch, and experiment if you're not happy. Note: In figure 4, the first side is shown behind and lighter than the second side.

1. Come out the end J toward the H on the next-to-last row. Go through it and continue through the K turn bead. Then go back through the J toward the edge. Make sure the clasp is oriented correctly and sew through the end loop from front to back (figure 4, orange dot and line on right).